RHODES ISLAND
TRAVEL GU

Copyright Notice

© 2024 [Dashel Eberhard Jr.]. All rights reserved.

No part of this travel guide may be reproduced, distributed, or transmitted in any form or by any means, including photocopying, recording, or other electronic or mechanical methods, without the prior written permission of the publisher, except in the case of brief quotations embodied in critical reviews and certain other noncommercial uses permitted by copyright law.

Disclaimer

The information provided in this Rhodes Island travel guide is intended to be used for general planning and informational purposes only. While we have made every effort to ensure the accuracy and reliability of the content, users should always verify specific details, opening hours, pricing, and availability of attractions, accommodations, transportation, and other services directly with the respective providers.

CONTENTS

Unlocking the Wonders of Rhodes 1

    Welcome to the Island of the Knights 2

    A Brief History of Rhodes 2

    Embracing the "Island of Roses" 3

Chapter 1: GETTING TO RHODES 4

    Air Travel to Rhodes 5

    Ferry Services to Rhodes 7

    Intermodal Connections 8

    Transportation Options on the Island 9

    Cost Ranges For Ferry And Air Travel To The Island Of Rhodes ... 10

    Air Travel Convenience and Flexibility 13

    Ferry Travel Convenience and Flexibility 14

Chapter 2: DIVERSE ACCOMMODATION CHOICES IN RHODES ... 16

    Immersive Old Town Boutique Hotels 17

    Luxurious Coastal Resorts 19

    Immersive Traditional Village Stays 20

Chapter 3: UNCOVERING THE ISLAND'S NATURAL WONDERS ... 24

    The Jewel in Rhodes' Crown: The Medieval Old Town 24

    The Palace of the Grand Master 25

    The Street of the Knights 25

The Seven Springs	26
The Acropolis of Lindos	27
The Valley of the Butterflies	28
The Rhodes Archaeological Museum: Guardians of the Island's Storied Past	29

Chapter 4: UNCOVERING THE ISLAND'S LESSER-KNOWN BUT FASCINATING HISTORICAL SITES — 31

The Kamiros Archaeological Site	31
The Monolithos Castle	32
The Ialyssos Archaeological Site	33
Guided Walks and Tours	34

Chapter 5: OUTDOOR ACTIVITIES: UNCOVERING THE ISLAND'S NATURAL WONDERS — 36

Hiking	37
Snorkeling	38

Chapter 7: CULINARY DELIGHTS ON THE ISLAND OF RHODES — 39

Seafood Specialties	40
Authentic Greek Cuisine	41
Olives, Cheeses, and Other Artisanal Delicacies	43
Dining Experiences	44
Must-Try Iconic Rhodian Dishes	46

Chapter 6: BEST TIME TO VISIT — 48

Summer 48
Spring and Autumn 49
Cultural Events & Festivals during These Seasons 50
Feast of St. John 50
Spring Festivals and Events 51
Autumn Festivals and Events 52
Religious Sites & Architecture 53

Chapter 8: TRADITIONAL ARTS AND CRAFTS OF RHODES FOR TOURISTS 55

- ✓ Visit the Old Town Artisan Workshops 56
- ✓ Attend Artisan Festivals and Demonstrations 56
- ✓ Explore Local Art Galleries and Shops 57
- ✓ Take a Hands-On Workshop or Class 57

Chapter 9: MUST-VISIT ARTISAN GALLERIES IN THE OLD TOWN OF RHODES 59

Ceramics Studios 59
Textile Workshops 60
Metal and Woodworking Shops 60
Fine Art Galleries 61
Heritage Shops 61

Chapter 10: CONCLUSION - RHODES, AN ENDURING ISLAND TREASURE 62

Reflections on the Island's Captivating Essence 62

Inspiration to Return and Explore Further	64
Preserving the Legacy of Rhodes	65
Practical Information	66
Dining and Nightlife	66
Shopping and Souvenirs	67
Health and Safety	68
Calendar of Events	69

Chapter 11: APPENDIX — 72

Rhodes Map	72
Suggested Itineraries	73
Useful Phrases in Greek	75
Additional Resources and References	75

Introduction

Unlocking the Wonders of Rhodes

Welcome to the enchanting island of Rhodes, a captivating destination that has captivated the hearts and imaginations of travelers for millennia. As you embark on your journey to this remarkable Greek isle, you will find yourself transported to a world where the past and present seamlessly intertwine, where natural beauty and cultural heritage converge to create an experience like no other.

Welcome to the Island of the Knights

Rhodes is a place steeped in history and legend, a testament to the enduring human spirit and the resilience of a people who have weathered the tides of time. From the imposing fortifications of the UNESCO-protected Medieval Old Town to the serene beaches that kiss the crystalline waters of the Aegean, this island's allure is undeniable. Here, you will walk in the footsteps of the Knights of St. John, explore the remnants of ancient civilizations, and immerse yourself in a vibrant living culture that has endured for millennia.

A Brief History of Rhodes

The history of Rhodes is a tapestry woven with the threads of conquest and resilience. Originally settled in the 16th century BC, the island has witnessed the rise and fall of empires, from the Dorians and the Persians to the Romans and the Byzantines. It was during the medieval era, however, that Rhodes truly captured the world's attention, as it became the stronghold of the Knights Hospitaller, who transformed the island into a formidable fortress and a center of trade and culture.

Embracing the "Island of Roses"

Despite the passage of time, Rhodes has retained its captivating essence, earning it the moniker "the Island of Roses." This enchanting destination continues to draw visitors from around the globe, each seeking to uncover the mysteries of its past, to bask in the beauty of its natural landscapes, and to immerse themselves in the warmth and hospitality of its people.

As you turn the pages of this travel guide, you will discover a wealth of information to help you unlock the secrets of Rhodes, from the hidden gems of the Old Town to the breathtaking natural wonders that dot the island's coastline. Whether you're seeking a cultural immersion, an outdoor adventure, or simply a chance to relax and rejuvenate, Rhodes offers an unparalleled experience that will leave an indelible mark on your heart and memories.

So, prepare to embark on a journey unlike any other, and let the wonders of Rhodes captivate your senses and ignite your spirit of exploration.

Chapter 1: GETTING TO RHODES

The island of Rhodes is a popular tourist destination located in the Aegean Sea, just off the southwestern coast of Turkey. Fortunately, Rhodes is easily accessible for travelers, with well-developed transportation options to reach the island from both domestic and international locations.

Air Travel to Rhodes

Rhodes International Airport (RHO) is the primary air gateway to the island, serving as a hub for both domestic and international flights. Located just 14 kilometers from the city of Rhodes, the airport handles a significant volume of both domestic and international flights throughout the year. The airport has undergone significant expansions and upgrades in recent years, making it a modern and well-equipped facility capable of handling the influx of visitors to Rhodes.

Major airlines operating direct flights to Rhodes include Aegean Airlines, Olympic Air, and a variety of European carriers such as Lufthansa, Air France, and British Airways. These airlines offer connections from many major cities across Europe, including London, Paris, Frankfurt, and Rome, as well as select destinations in the Middle East and North Africa. The flight duration from major European cities typically ranges from 2.5 to 4.5 hours, making Rhodes an easily accessible destination.

For travelers within Greece, Rhodes is well-connected to other domestic airports, with regular flights from Athens, Thessaloniki, and several regional hubs. These intra-country connections make it easy for visitors to incorporate Rhodes into a broader Greek itinerary.

Upon arrival, passengers will find a range of ground transportation options waiting to whisk them to their final destinations across the island. Taxis, shuttle buses, and car rental agencies are all readily available, ensuring a seamless and efficient transfer from the airport.

Ferry Services to Rhodes

In addition to air travel, Rhodes can also be accessed by sea, with the island's two main ports – the **Port of Rhodes** and the **Port of Mandraki** – serving as important maritime hubs.

The Port of Rhodes, situated in the heart of the city, is the primary port for passenger ferries and cruise ships. It connects Rhodes to various destinations in Greece, including Piraeus (the port of Athens), as well as to islands in the Dodecanese archipelago and the nearby Turkish ports of Marmaris and Bodrum.

The Port of Mandraki, located just a short distance from the Old Town, predominantly handles cargo ships and private yachts. This picturesque harbor, with its iconic deer statues, also serves as a departure point for day trips and excursions to nearby islands.

Travelers can choose from a variety of ferry operators and schedules, with journey times ranging from a few hours to overnight crossings, depending on the departure point and the type of vessel.

Intermodal Connections

For those looking to combine air and sea travel, Rhodes offers excellent intermodal connectivity. Visitors can easily fly into the island's airport and then utilize the ferry system to explore neighboring destinations, or vice versa, creating a well-rounded and flexible travel itinerary.

The island's transportation network is designed to facilitate seamless transitions between different modes of travel, ensuring that visitors can navigate Rhodes and its surrounding region with ease.

Overall, the comprehensive transportation options available to Rhodes, from efficient air links to scenic maritime routes, make the island highly accessible and convenient for travelers from both near and far. Whether arriving by plane or by boat, visitors can look forward to a smooth and enjoyable start to their Rhodes adventure.

Transportation Options on the Island

Once you've arrived on the island, you'll find that Rhodes offers a well-developed transportation network to help you explore its diverse landscapes and attractions.

- Rental Cars

Renting a car is an excellent way to enjoy the freedom and flexibility to discover Rhodes at your own pace. The island's road network is well-maintained, and car rental agencies can be found throughout the major towns and tourist hubs.

- Public Buses

Rhodes boasts an extensive network of public buses, known as "RODA" (Rhodes Public Transport), that connect the main towns and villages. This affordable and convenient option allows you to navigate the island without the hassle of driving.

- Taxis

Taxis are readily available, especially in the larger towns and around major tourist sites. They provide a comfortable and direct way to get around, particularly for shorter trips or if you have heavy luggage.

- Bicycles and E-Bikes

Exploring Rhodes by bicycle or electric bicycle is a popular and eco-friendly way to discover the island's scenic coastal roads, quaint villages, and hidden gems. Many rental shops and tour operators offer bike rentals and guided cycling tours.

- Ferries and Boats

For those interested in island-hopping or coastal excursions, the island's ferry and boat services provide easy access to nearby islands and destinations along the coastline.

Whether you opt for the convenience of a rental car, the efficiency of public transportation, or the adventure of cycling, Rhodes offers a variety of transportation options to suit your preferences and travel style.

Cost Ranges For Ferry And Air Travel To The Island Of Rhodes:

- **Ferry Costs**

Traveling to Rhodes by ferry can be a cost-effective option, especially for those already in the Greek islands or along the Turkish coast.

Domestic Greek Ferry Routes:

- From Kos: €15 - €30 one-way
- From Symi: €10 - €20 one-way

International Ferry Routes:

- From Marmaris, Turkey: €20 - €40 one-way

Prices can vary depending on the ferry operator, vessel type, and amenities. Overnight or high-speed ferry services tend to be more expensive than slower, conventional ferries.

- **Air Travel Costs**

Flying to Rhodes is generally the faster and more convenient option, but can also be more expensive, especially for international travelers.

Domestic Flights within Greece:

- From Athens: €50 - €100 one-way
- From Thessaloniki: €80 - €150 one-way

International Flights:

- From London: €150 - €300 round-trip
- From Paris: €200 - €400 round-trip
- From Frankfurt: €200 - €400 round-trip

Airfares can fluctuate significantly based on the airline, season, and booking lead time. Budget airlines and advance bookings can help travelers find more affordable options.

It's worth noting that costs may also include additional fees for things like checked baggage, seat selection, and in-flight services, so it's important to factor these into the total travel budget.

Ultimately, the choice between ferry or air travel will depend on the traveler's budget, schedule, and preferred mode of transport. Both options provide convenient access to the island of Rhodes for visitors.

When comparing the convenience and flexibility of ferry versus air travel options for getting to Rhodes, there are some key differences to consider:

Air Travel Convenience and Flexibility

- **Faster Journeys**

Flights to Rhodes from most major European and Greek hubs take just 1-2 hours, whereas ferry journeys can take several hours, depending on the origin.

- **Frequent Schedules**

There are multiple daily flight options to Rhodes from the main Greek airports, providing ample flexibility for travelers' schedules.

- **Wider Connectivity**

The island's international airport allows for direct connections from a broad range of European and Middle Eastern cities, making it accessible from a greater number of origin points.

- **Streamlined Arrivals:**

Disembarking at the airport allows for a quicker and more efficient transfer to final destinations across Rhodes, compared to ferry terminals.

Ferry Travel Convenience and Flexibility

- **Scenic Journeys**

Traveling to Rhodes by ferry offers the opportunity to enjoy the beautiful coastal scenery of the Aegean Sea, which can be a highlight of the trip for some travelers.

- **Flexibility for Island Hopping**

For those wishing to visit multiple Greek islands, the ferry network provides the flexibility to incorporate Rhodes into a broader island-hopping itinerary.

- **Lower Costs**

Ferries are generally a more budget-friendly option compared to flights, especially for domestic Greek routes.

- **Convenient Terminal Locations**

The main ferry terminals on Rhodes are situated directly in the capital city, making onward travel within the island straightforward.

In summary, air travel offers faster, more frequent, and better-connected options, catering to travelers seeking an efficient and convenient means of reaching Rhodes. However, the ferry system provides a more scenic and flexible mode of transportation, particularly for those interested in exploring the broader Greek islands region.

Ultimately, the choice between air or ferry travel will depend on the individual traveler's priorities, budget, and the overall structure of their Rhodes and Greek itinerary.

Chapter 2: DIVERSE ACCOMMODATION CHOICES IN RHODES

When planning a visit to the stunning Greek island of Rhodes, travelers are presented with a vast array of accommodation options, each offering a unique experience catered to a wide range of preferences and budgets. From historic boutique hotels nestled within the captivating Medieval Old Town to expansive coastal resorts and charming traditional village stays, Rhodes ensures that every visitor can find the perfect fit for their desired vacation experience.

Immersive Old Town Boutique Hotels

Tucked away within the well-preserved walls of the UNESCO-listed Medieval Old Town, a collection of charming boutique hotels provides visitors with an immersive and historic stay. These intimate properties, often housed in beautifully restored traditional buildings, seamlessly blend modern comforts with the architectural and cultural heritage of this timeless destination.

Guests staying in the Old Town boutique hotels can expect personalized service, thoughtfully designed guest rooms, and easy access to the winding cobblestone streets, centuries-old landmarks, lively cafes, and thriving artisan workshops that define the Old Town's captivating ambiance. Many of these properties feature inviting rooftop terraces or tranquil courtyards, offering stunning views of the surrounding historic structures and capturing the essence of Rhodes' medieval past.

Some of the Old Town Boutique Hotels:

- **Hotel Anexartisia**

Located in the heart of the Old Town, this 16th-century mansion has been meticulously renovated, preserving its original architectural features while providing modern amenities. Rates start at €150 per night.

- Melenos Lindos

This stunning boutique hotel in the charming village of Lindos features whitewashed walls, traditional Greek furnishings, and stunning views of the Acropolis. Rates range from €180 to €300 per night.

- Ferarri Boutique Hotel

Situated along the Street of the Knights, this intimate hotel offers just 12 elegantly appointed rooms, transporting guests back to the era of the Knights Hospitaller. Rates start at €200 per night.

- Kypriotis Boutique Hotel

An intimate 8-room property housed in a historic building, offering elegant decor and a rooftop terrace overlooking the medieval streets. Rates are typically between €180 to €280 per night.

- Odysseus Boutique Hotel

This 20-room hotel is set in a beautifully preserved 14th-century structure, with a focus on personalized service and traditional Greek design elements. Nightly rates generally fall within the €200 to €400 range.

Luxurious Coastal Resorts

For travelers seeking a more resort-style vacation, Rhodes boasts an impressive selection of premium properties located along its picturesque Mediterranean coastline. These expansive, full-service resorts offer direct access to private sandy beaches, as well as an abundance of amenities to cater to a wide range of needs and preferences.

From multiple swimming pools and water sports facilities to diverse dining options, indulgent spa centers, and dedicated family-friendly or adults-only zones, these coastal retreats provide a hassle-free and luxurious holiday experience. Many of the resorts also feature dedicated children's clubs and age-appropriate activities, ensuring that families can enjoy a seamless and enjoyable stay.

Some of the Luxurious Coastal Resorts:

- Lindos Princess Beach Hotel

A sprawling 5-star resort with direct beach access, multiple pools, 8 restaurants, a spa, and dedicated family and adult-only zones. All-inclusive rates start around €300 per person per night during high season. Address: Krana, Lindos 85107, Greece.

- Rodos Palladium Leisure & Wellness

This luxurious all-inclusive resort features an impressive array of amenities, including water sports facilities, kids' clubs, and an award-winning spa. Rates range from €400 to €600 per night for a standard room, with higher prices for suites. Address: Ixia, Rhodes 85101, Greece.

- Sheraton Rhodes Resort

A premium beachfront resort with modern guest rooms, 6 restaurants, 4 bars, and a variety of recreational activities and entertainment. Room rates are in the €250 to €500 per night bracket, with premium beachfront rooms at the higher end. Address: Ialyssos Ave, Rhodes 85100, Greece.

- Ixian All Suites

This all-inclusive resort in Ixia features spacious suites, multiple pools, and a private beach. Rates start at €300 per night, with all-inclusive packages available.

- Atrium Platinum Luxury Resort & Spa

Located in Ialyssos, this opulent resort features a private beach, infinity pool, and world-class spa. Rates range from €500 to €800 per night.

Immersive Traditional Village Stays

Beyond the coastal areas and the captivating Old Town, Rhodes is home to a network of charming traditional villages that offer visitors a unique and immersive accommodation experience. These off-the-beaten-path options range from converted stone houses and family-run guesthouses to agritourism properties, providing guests with the opportunity to fully immerse themselves in the island's local culture and rural way of life.

Visitors staying in these traditional village accommodations can expect a more intimate setting, the chance to participate in authentic local activities, and the opportunity to savor homemade regional cuisine, all while surrounded by the natural beauty of the island's hinterland. The small scale of these properties allows for meaningful interactions and exchanges with the Greek families who own and operate them, fostering a deeper understanding of the daily lives, customs, and traditions of the villagers.

Some of the Traditional Village Stays:

- **Archontiko Paliokaloyrou**

A historic mansion-turned-guesthouse in the picturesque village of Embonas, offering authentic Greek hospitality and opportunities to learn about local winemaking. Room rates are approximately €120 to €180 per night.

Address: Embonas, Rhodes 85107, Greece.

- Kamiros Suites

These charming stone-built suites in the village of Kalavarda provide a peaceful escape, with options for cooking classes and olive oil tastings. Nightly rates for the suites typically fall between €150 to €250.

Address: Kalavarda, Rhodes 85104, Greece.

- Melenos Lindos

A renowned boutique hotel in the medieval hilltop village of Lindos, featuring traditional Rhodian architecture and hosting regular cultural events. Expect to pay €300 to €500 per night at this boutique village hotel.

Address: Lindos 85107, Greece.

- Kritinia Village Guesthouse

This family-run guesthouse in the picturesque village of Kritinia offers a taste of authentic Greek hospitality, with rates starting at €80 per night.

- Archipolis Suites

Situated in the quaint village of Embonas, known for its wine production, these traditional suites provide a peaceful and authentic island escape. Rates range from €100 to €150 per night.

- Kastellos Traditional Guesthouse

Located in the hillside village of Kastellos, this charming guesthouse offers stunning views and a glimpse into the island's rural heritage. Rates start at €90 per night.

Regardless of the accommodation style, Rhodes ensures that every traveler can find the perfect fit for their preferences, budget, and the type of experience they hope to have during their visit to this captivating Dodecanese island.

Chapter 3: UNCOVERING THE ISLAND'S NATURAL WONDERS

As one of the largest and most historically significant islands in Greece, Rhodes boasts an abundance of captivating sites and landmarks that have enchanted visitors for centuries. From the perfectly preserved medieval wonders of the Old Town to ancient archaeological ruins, natural havens, and world-class museums, the island's diverse array of attractions offers something to enthrall every type of traveler.

The Jewel in Rhodes' Crown: The Medieval Old Town

At the heart of the island's allure lies the remarkably intact Old Town of Rhodes, a UNESCO World Heritage Site that transports visitors back to the era of the Knights Hospitaller. Wandering the labyrinthine streets, travelers are enveloped by the imposing limestone walls, Gothic architecture, and the charming squares and fountains that have stood the test of time.

The Palace of the Grand Master

One of the most iconic landmarks is the Palace of the Grand Master, a formidable 14th-century citadel that once housed the leaders of the Knights of Saint John. Today, the palace's exquisitely restored halls and chambers showcase a treasure trove of Byzantine and medieval artifacts, including colorful mosaics, intricate tapestries, and ornate furnishings that offer a glimpse into the opulent lives of the knights.

The Street of the Knights

Another highlight is the picturesque Street of the Knights, a meticulously preserved thoroughfare lined with the former lodgings of the knights, each adorned with the heraldic shields and crests of the different langues, or tongues, of the Order. As visitors stroll down this historic avenue, they can almost hear the echoes of the knights' footsteps and imagine the clatter of hooves as they prepared to defend the island from invaders.

Scattered throughout the Old Town, the stunning Byzantine churches also captivate the senses, with their dazzling interiors of glittering mosaics, sacred icons, and elaborate frescoes. One of the most remarkable is the Church of Our Lady of the Castle, perched atop the highest point of the medieval city and offering sweeping views of the surrounding historic district and the shimmering Aegean beyond.

The Seven Springs

Tucked away in the lush, verdant hills of the island's interior, the Seven Springs (Epta Piges) is a captivating natural wonder that offers a welcome respite from the bustling towns and sun-drenched beaches of Rhodes.

As you approach this enchanting oasis, you'll be immediately struck by the serene atmosphere and the soothing sound of flowing water. The Seven Springs are, as the name suggests, a cluster of seven natural springs that converge to form a tranquil stream, winding its way through a densely forested gorge.

Take a leisurely stroll along the shaded paths, admiring the vibrant greenery and the crystal-clear pools that dot the landscape. Marvel at the intricate system of stone bridges and aqueducts that have channeled the springs' waters for centuries, a testament to the ingenuity of the island's inhabitants.

Pause for a moment at one of the picturesque rest areas, where you can dip your feet in the cool, refreshing waters and escape the heat of the Mediterranean sun. As you listen to the soothing sounds of the springs, let your mind wander and your senses be enveloped by the serene natural beauty that surrounds you.

The Seven Springs is not just a stunning natural attraction; it is also a hub of cultural and historical significance. Explore the nearby abandoned water mills and learn about the important role that this water source has played in the island's agricultural and industrial development over the centuries.

Whether you're seeking a peaceful respite, a unique natural experience, or a chance to connect with the island's rich heritage, a visit to the Seven Springs is sure to leave a lasting impression on your Rhodes adventure.

The Acropolis of Lindos

Perched atop a towering rocky outcrop on the island's eastern coast, the Acropolis of Lindos stands as one of Greece's most breathtaking archaeological sites. Visitors can climb the steep stone steps leading up to the ancient ruins, which include the well-preserved Temple of Athena Lindia, the remains of a medieval castle, and panoramic views stretching out over the sparkling Aegean Sea.

According to mythology, the acropolis was the site of a temple dedicated to the goddess Athena, who was revered by the ancient Rhodians. Over the centuries, the site evolved, with the temple being rebuilt and expanded by successive rulers, including the Dorians, the Persians, and the knights of St. John. The remains of these different architectural styles can be seen in the various columns, doorways, and other structural elements that dot the site.

As travelers ascend the ancient stairway, they are rewarded not only with the awe-inspiring views, but also with the opportunity to imagine the colorful history that has unfolded on this hallowed ground. Local guides often regale visitors with tales of the site's strategic importance, the battles that were fought here, and the rituals and ceremonies that took place in the shadow of the temple of Athena.

The Valley of the Butterflies

Located in the lush, mountainous interior of Rhodes, the Valley of the Butterflies is a natural wonder unlike any other. During the summer months, this verdant, shaded canyon plays host to millions of the protected Panaxia quadripunctaria butterfly, whose vibrant orange and black wings create a mesmerizing spectacle.

Visitors can wander along the wooden walkways, observe the butterflies in their natural habitat, and immerse themselves in the serene, almost otherworldly ambiance of this unique ecological refuge. The valley's microclimate, with its cool, humid air and abundant water sources, provides the ideal conditions for the butterflies to thrive, drawn to the area's diverse flora and the tranquil, shaded environment.

Beyond the butterflies, the Valley of the Butterflies is also home to a diverse array of other flora and fauna, including towering plane trees, babbling brooks, and a variety of bird species. Hikers can explore the network of trails that wind through the verdant landscape, pausing to dip their feet in the refreshing pools or to enjoy a picnic lunch amid the serene natural surroundings.

The Rhodes Archaeological Museum: Guardians of the Island's Storied Past

As the repository of the island's impressive Greek, Roman, and Byzantine history, the Rhodes Archaeological Museum is an essential stop for cultural enthusiasts. The museum's rich collection includes intricate mosaics, ancient sculptures, pottery, and other artifacts that tell the captivating story of Rhodes' strategic importance and artistic legacy over the centuries.

One of the museum's most iconic pieces is the Colossus of Rhodes, a towering statue that was once one of the Seven Wonders of the Ancient World. Though the original statue was destroyed by an earthquake in the 3rd century BCE, the museum displays a scale model that gives visitors a sense of the statue's massive scale and grandeur. Alongside this iconic relic, the museum also houses the stunning Aphrodite of Rhodes, a breathtaking Hellenistic sculpture that is considered one of the finest examples of ancient Greek art.

As visitors wander through the museum's meticulously curated galleries, they are transported back in time, immersing themselves in the rich cultural tapestry that has defined Rhodes for millennia. Knowledgeable docents are on hand to share the fascinating stories behind the artifacts, bringing the island's history to life and inspiring a deeper appreciation for the enduring legacy of this remarkable Greek destination.

Chapter 4: UNCOVERING THE ISLAND'S LESSER-KNOWN BUT FASCINATING HISTORICAL SITES

The Kamiros Archaeological Site

Situated on the island's northwest coast, the ancient city of Kamiros is one of Rhodes' most significant yet underrated archaeological treasures. Once a thriving Doric city-state, Kamiros reached the height of its prosperity in the 5th century BCE before being gradually abandoned over the centuries. Today, the extensive excavations reveal the remarkably well-preserved ruins of houses, shops, temples, and public buildings that offer a tangible glimpse into the daily life of ancient Rhodians.

As visitors wander through the atmospheric ruins, they can imagine the bustling marketplace, the processions to the temples, and the lively intellectual discourse that would have filled the streets of this prosperous ancient city. Highlights include the imposing remains of the Doric temple complex, the elaborately decorated tombs, and the stunning views overlooking the sparkling Aegean Sea. Often bypassed by the crowds flocking to Lindos or the medieval Old Town, Kamiros provides a quieter, more contemplative window into Rhodes' ancient past.

The Monolithos Castle

Perched atop a towering 236-meter-high rock outcrop on the island's western coast, the imposing ruins of Monolithos Castle command panoramic views over the Aegean. Originally constructed in the 15th century by the Knights of St. John, the castle was built as a defensive fortification to guard against pirate raids and Ottoman incursions.

Though much of the original structure has crumbled over the centuries, the castle's dramatic setting and the remnants of its thick stone walls and towers still evoke a strong sense of historical grandeur. Visitors who make the winding ascent up the steep path to the castle ruins are rewarded not only with stunning vistas, but also with the opportunity to imagine the castle in its heyday, when it served as a vital outpost for the knights as they sought to defend their island stronghold.

While less famous than the medieval Old Town, Monolithos Castle offers a more off-the-beaten-path historical experience, allowing travelers to discover Rhodes' multilayered past in a more tranquil and contemplative setting.

The Ialyssos Archaeological Site

Often overshadowed by the more famous ruins of Kamiros and Lindos, the archaeological site of Ialyssos is another hidden gem that offers a fascinating glimpse into Rhodes' Hellenistic and Roman history. Situated on the island's northern coast, the site was once home to one of the three ancient city-states that dominated Rhodes in antiquity.

Visitors can explore the remains of Ialyssos' ancient acropolis, which was fortified with massive defensive walls, as well as the ruins of temples, public buildings, and residential structures that give a sense of the city's former grandeur. One of the highlights is the well-preserved gymnasium complex, where ancient Rhodians would have gathered to exercise, socialize, and engage in intellectual pursuits.

While the site may lack the sheer scale and dramatic setting of some of Rhodes' other archaeological treasures, Ialyssos nonetheless offers a more intimate and immersive experience, allowing travelers to wander among the evocative ruins and imagine the bustling urban life that once thrived in this corner of the island. With fewer crowds than the more famous sites, Ialyssos provides a peaceful respite for history buffs seeking to delve deeper into Rhodes' captivating past.

Guided Walks and Tours

To truly immerse yourself in the rich history and cultural heritage of the Medieval Old Town, consider joining one of the guided walking tours or themed excursions offered by local experts.

These knowledgeable guides will lead you through the winding streets, regaling you with tales of the Knights, the sieges, and the everyday life of the island's inhabitants throughout the centuries. As you explore the hidden alleyways, discover the architectural marvels, and uncover the secrets of the past, you'll gain a deeper understanding and appreciation for the layers of history that have shaped this remarkable destination.

Whether you opt for a general tour of the Old Town or a more specialized exploration focused on a particular aspect of its history, such as the Knights' defensive systems or the island's

Byzantine heritage, you're sure to come away with a newfound appreciation for the enduring legacy of the Medieval Old Town.

Engaging with the local community, discovering hidden gems, and immersing yourself in the sights, sounds, and stories of the past – these are the hallmarks of a truly memorable guided tour in the Medieval Old Town of Rhodes.

Chapter 5: OUTDOOR ACTIVITIES: UNCOVERING THE ISLAND'S NATURAL WONDERS

As one of the largest and most geographically diverse Greek islands, Rhodes offers visitors a wealth of opportunities to experience its natural wonders through a variety of outdoor pursuits. From challenging hikes through lush, mountainous terrain to leisurely water-based activities along the picturesque coastline, the island caters to adventure-seekers and nature enthusiasts alike.

Hiking

Rhodes' diverse landscapes provide ample hiking opportunities, with trails ranging from easy, scenic walks to more strenuous ascents offering panoramic vistas. One of the island's most iconic hiking destinations is the Valley of the Butterflies, a nature reserve renowned for the millions of brightly colored Callimorpha moths that migrate there each summer. Visitors can meander along shaded forest paths, catching glimpses of the delicate insects fluttering among the lush vegetation.

Forms:

- **Trails through the Valley of the Butterflies**

This unique nature reserve is home to millions of colorful Callimorpha butterflies that migrate to the valley each summer, creating a mesmerizing natural spectacle. Hiking through the lush, verdant landscapes, visitors can spot these delicate insects fluttering among the trees and pause to admire the serene, shaded gorges.

- **Paths along the Profitis Ilias mountain range**

Offering panoramic vistas of the Aegean Sea, the Profitis Ilias mountain range features a network of well-marked hiking trails that range in difficulty from leisurely strolls to more challenging ascents. One popular route leads hikers to the summit of Mount Attavyros, the island's highest peak at 1,215 meters, where on a clear day one can see as far as the coast of Turkey.

- Coastal hikes with dramatic sea views

Rhodes' perimeter is dotted with picturesque seaside trails that wind along cliffsides and rocky promontories, providing hikers with awe-inspiring views of the island's craggy coastline and the sparkling Aespot wildlife like fish and sea turtles up close

Snorkeling

- The excellent visibility in the waters around Rhodes makes it an ideal destination for snorkeling

- Even without diving experience, you can use a mask and snorkel to explore the vibrant underwater world just below the surface

- Popular snorkeling spots include sheltered bays and coves, where you can observe colorful fish, sea urchins, and other marine life

These water-based activities provide first-time visitors a unique and memorable way to fully immerse themselves in Rhodes' breathtaking coastal landscapes. The availability of guided tours and equipment rentals makes these experiences accessible for travelers of all skill levels.

Chapter 7: CULINARY DELIGHTS ON THE ISLAND OF RHODES

The island of Rhodes has long been revered as a gastronomic paradise, where the bountiful local ingredients, time-honored cooking traditions, and diverse cultural influences converge to create an unparalleled dining experience. From the fresh-caught seafood plucked straight from the sparkling Aegean waters to the hearty, flavor-packed recipes that have been passed down through generations, the flavors of Rhodes captivate the senses and leave a lasting impression on every visitor.

Seafood Specialties

As an island nation, it should come as no surprise that seafood is a culinary cornerstone of Rhodes. The strategic coastal location of the island means that the daily catches of local fishermen feature an incredible array of marine delicacies, from the vibrant red mullet and briny octopus to the succulent sea bream and glistening sardines. These abundant seafood offerings are prepared in a variety of mouthwatering ways, showcasing the culinary ingenuity of the island's chefs.

One beloved local dish is the lakerda, a traditional cured fish specialty that originated in the Dodecanese islands. To create this delicacy, fresh bonito or amberjack fillets are salted and dried in the warm Mediterranean sun, resulting in a firm, intensely flavorful end product that is often shaved thin and served as an appetizer or meze. Another iconic Rhodian seafood preparation is the kalamari, or fried calamari, which features local squid or octopus lightly dusted in flour and fried to golden perfection. These crispy, tender morsels are frequently paired with a zesty lemon wedge or a tangy tzatziki sauce for dipping.

For a true taste of the sea, visitors flock to the island's picturesque harbors and seaside tavernas to savor just-caught fish grilled over hot coals. Chefs take great pride in selecting the freshest and most pristine specimens, allowing the natural flavors of the seafood to shine. Favorites include the branzino (European sea bass), tsipoura (gilt-head bream), and barbounia (red mullet), which are often simply seasoned with lemon, olive oil, and aromatic herbs.

Beyond these classic seafood preparations, the culinary creativity of Rhodes also shines through in innovative dishes that blend local maritime ingredients with global influences. At upscale restaurants in Rhodes Town, diners may encounter delicacies such as octopus carpaccio, crayfish ravioli, or sea urchin risotto - masterful compositions that showcase the island's gastronomy in a modern, elevated light.

Authentic Greek Cuisine

While seafood undoubtedly reigns supreme, the island of Rhodes is also renowned for its exceptional Greek cuisine, which draws upon the rich culinary heritage of the region. Iconic dishes such as moussaka, dolmades, and spanakopita grace menus across the island, showcasing the depth and complexity of Rhodian gastronomy.

One of the standout specialties of Rhodes is the island's take on the classic Greek salad, or horiatiki. Unlike the ubiquitous renditions found throughout the country, the Rhodian horiatiki features locally grown tomatoes, cucumbers, and onions, as well as capers, olives, and blocks of creamy feta cheese sourced directly from the island's producers. Drizzled with a generous pour of pungent, golden extra-virgin olive oil, this quintessential Greek salad is a refreshing and flavorful celebration of the island's bountiful natural resources.

Another beloved Rhodian dish is the gemista, which consists of vine leaves, peppers, or tomatoes stuffed with a savory rice and herb filling. The labor-intensive preparation of these delectable parcels is a true testament to the culinary traditions of the island, with families often gathering together to carefully assemble each individual serving. When accompanied by a side of crisp roasted potatoes, the gemista embodies the comforting, family-style essence of Greek cuisine.

No exploration of Rhodian gastronomy would be complete without mentioning the renowned moussaka, a layered casserole made with eggplant, ground meat, and a rich béchamel sauce. While this dish is found throughout Greece, the version hailing from Rhodes is often distinguished by the addition of local cheeses and a more pronounced use of spices like cinnamon and allspice. Savored fresh from the oven, the moussaka's fragrant aromas and creamy, satisfying textures are sure to delight the senses.

Beyond these iconic staples, the island's culinary culture also encompasses a wealth of other traditional specialties. Visitors can sample hearty bean stews, delicate dolmades (stuffed grape leaves), and flaky spanakopita (spinach and feta pies) - each prepared with care and reverence for the recipes that have been passed down through generations.

Olives, Cheeses, and Other Artisanal Delicacies

No culinary exploration of Rhodes would be complete without indulging in the island's exceptional olives and cheeses, which are considered among the finest in all of Greece. The mild Mediterranean climate and fertile soil of Rhodes create the ideal conditions for producing a bounty of artisanal food products that reflect the unique terroir of the region.

Chief among these local delicacies are the pungent, briny Dodecanese olives, which are pressed into rich, golden extra-virgin olive oil. Visitors can sample these flavorful olives on their own, as well as incorporated into traditional dishes and salads. The island is also renowned for its specialty cheeses, such as the creamy, tangy local feta and the firm, nutty graviera. These artisanal dairy products are often served as part of meze platters, drizzled with honey, or used as key ingredients in cooked dishes.

In addition to olives and cheeses, Rhodes boasts a variety of other artisanal food products that are worth seeking out. The island is home to an abundance of citrus orchards, which yield exceptionally fragrant and juicy lemons, oranges, and mandarins. These vibrant fruits are not only used in cooking, but also feature prominently in the island's selection of refreshing herbal teas and signature cocktails. The local honey, harvested from the nectar of the island's diverse wildflowers, is another prized Rhodian delicacy, often served alongside traditional desserts or drizzled over fresh Greek yogurt.

For those interested in exploring the full breadth of the island's artisanal food scene, a visit to one of Rhodes' bustling local markets or specialty food shops is a must. Here, visitors can engage directly with the passionate producers and purveyors who take great pride in sharing the stories and traditions behind their exceptional wares.

Dining Experiences

To truly immerse oneself in the culinary culture of Rhodes, travelers are encouraged to seek out family-owned restaurants and local eateries that prioritize the use of fresh, locally-sourced ingredients and time-honored cooking methods. These establishments offer an unparalleled opportunity to connect with the island's gastronomic heritage, as diners can engage with the passionate chefs and servers who take great pride in sharing their recipes and stories.

In the charming villages that dot the Rhodian countryside, visitors may stumble upon hidden gem tavernas that have been family-owned for generations. Here, long-held recipes for classic Greek dishes like moussaka and gemista are prepared with meticulous care, often using produce and proteins sourced directly from the proprietors' own gardens and farms. The informal, convivial atmosphere of these local eateries fosters a sense of community and cultural exchange, as diners can learn about the island's traditions while savoring the flavors of Rhodes.

For a more upscale dining experience, the island's coastal cities, such as Rhodes Town and Lindos, offer a wealth of sophisticated restaurants that showcase the culinary creativity of a new generation of Rhodian chefs. These establishments blend classic Greek flavors with modern culinary techniques, resulting in innovative dishes that delight the senses. Diners may encounter inspired takes on traditional meze platters, artisanal cocktails infused with local herbs and citrus, or gourmet interpretations of beloved desserts like baklava and yogurt with honey.

No culinary exploration of Rhodes would be complete without a taste of the island's renowned wines. The vineyards of Rhodes have been producing distinctive, aromatic white and red wines for centuries, with varietals like Assyrtiko and Mandilaria showcasing the unique terroir of the region.

Whether you're savoring a fresh seafood platter, indulging in a hearty Greek casserole, or sipping a glass of local wine, a gastronomic journey through Rhodes promises to delight the senses and transport you to the heart of the Aegean. It's a destination that celebrates the timeless traditions and vibrant flavors of Greek cuisine.

Must-Try Iconic Rhodian Dishes

Below are of some of the most popular and finest Rhodian dishes that visitors to the island should be sure to try:

Maridaki (Fried Small Fish): A classic Rhodian appetizer, this dish features a variety of small, locally caught fish that are lightly fried and often served with a tangy lemon-garlic sauce.

Gemista (Stuffed Tomatoes and Peppers): A quintessential Greek dish, Rhodian gemista are hallmarked by their use of the island's prized local tomatoes and peppers, which are stuffed with a savory rice and ground meat filling.

Moussaka: This beloved Greek casserole features layers of eggplant, ground beef or lamb, and a rich béchamel sauce. Rhodian versions often incorporate local ingredients like Ladotyri cheese and fresh herbs.

Rhopoulos (Fried Squid): Tender, lightly fried squid is a Rhodian specialty, often served as a meze (appetizer) or as a main course accompanied by lemon wedges and tzatziki sauce.

Dolmades (Stuffed Grape Leaves): These elegant, bite-sized delicacies feature grape leaves stuffed with a fragrant mixture of rice, herbs, and sometimes ground meat.

Rhodian Salad: A refreshing take on the classic Greek salad, the Rhodian version features the island's juicy tomatoes, crisp cucumbers, sharp red onions, briny olives, and creamy feta cheese, all dressed in the region's peppery olive oil.

Pastourmas (Cured, Spiced Meat): A unique Rhodian charcuterie item, pastourmas is a cured, air-dried meat that is seasoned with a blend of spices, garlic, and fenugreek.

Rhodian Wine: No culinary exploration of the island would be complete without sampling the distinctive local wines, such as the crisp, mineral-driven white wines made from the Assyrtiko grape or the bold, fruit-forward reds crafted from the Mandilaria varietal.

These are just a few of the many delectable dishes and ingredients that make Rhodian cuisine so special and worth exploring for any visitor to the island. By immersing themselves in the flavors of Rhodes, travelers can gain a deeper appreciation for the island's rich culinary heritage and the dedication of its food producers.

Chapter 6: BEST TIME TO VISIT

When it comes to the best time to experience the enchanting island of Rhodes, visitors have a few ideal windows to choose from throughout the year.

Summer

The summer months of June through August are undoubtedly the most popular time for travelers to visit Rhodes. With long, sunny days, warm Mediterranean temperatures, and minimal rainfall, the summer season offers the quintessential Greek island experience. Beachgoers can take advantage of the crystal-clear waters along the island's stunning coastlines, while adventurous visitors can explore ancient ruins, hike through scenic landscapes, and immerse themselves in the vibrant cultural events that enliven the island during the peak tourism season.

However, it's important to note that the summer months also bring larger crowds, higher accommodation prices, and increased demand for popular attractions. Those seeking a more tranquil atmosphere may want to consider visiting Rhodes during the shoulder seasons.

Spring and Autumn

The shoulder seasons of spring (March-May) and autumn (September-November) can be equally rewarding times to explore Rhodes. During these periods, visitors can enjoy milder temperatures, fewer crowds, and lower prices on flights and lodging. The spring months in particular offer the chance to witness the island's landscapes in bloom, with lush greenery, wildflowers, and almond trees in full blossom. Autumn, on the other hand, is an excellent time for hiking, as the temperatures cool and the crowds thin out.

While the swimming season may be slightly shorter during the spring and autumn, these shoulder seasons still offer ample opportunities to enjoy Rhodes' beaches, cultural sites, and outdoor activities without the intensity of the summer heat. Additionally, many local festivals and events take place during the spring and fall, providing visitors with a more immersive cultural experience.

Ultimately, the best time to visit Rhodes depends on the traveler's priorities and preferences. Whether it's the vibrant energy of summer, the blooming landscapes of spring, or the tranquil ambiance of autumn, Rhodes offers a wealth of experiences for visitors to discover throughout the year.

Cultural Events & Festivals during These Seasons

Immerse yourself in the vibrant cultural life of Rhodes by participating in the island's lively festivals and celebrations, which offer a unique glimpse into the traditions, customs, and values that have been passed down through generations. Cultural events and festivals that take place in Rhodes during the spring and autumn seasons include:

Feast of St. John

One of the island's most renowned cultural events is the Feast of St. John, a week-long celebration that takes place every

June in the medieval Old Town of Rhodes. Witness the colorful parades, traditional music and dance performances, and lively street markets that bring the historic district to life, and join the local community in honoring the patron saint of the Knights Hospitaller.

For a truly immersive experience, attend the annual Hellenic Festival, a celebration of Greek culture that takes place throughout the summer months. Enjoy live music and dance performances, sample traditional Rhodian cuisine, and explore the artisanal workshops that showcase the island's rich heritage of handicrafts and artistry.

Spring Festivals and Events

As the island awakens from the winter months, Rhodes plays host to a variety of lively cultural celebrations in the spring:

- **Rhodes Medieval Festival (April-May):**

This annual event transforms the medieval Old Town into a living museum, with reenactments, musical performances, and artisanal demonstrations that immerse visitors in the island's rich history.

- **Rhodian Wine Festival (May):**

Held in the picturesque town of Kamiros, this festival celebrates the island's thriving wine culture, allowing visitors to sample local vintages, attend tastings, and learn about the region's unique viticulture.

- Greek Orthodox Easter (April/May):

Though the exact date varies each year, the vibrant celebrations of Greek Orthodox Easter bring the island to life, with traditional processions, feasts, and religious ceremonies that offer insight into Rhodian customs.

Autumn Festivals and Events

As the summer crowds begin to dissipate, Rhodes embraces a more tranquil, introspective atmosphere in the autumn, highlighted by a number of cultural events:

- Rhodes International Film Festival (September-October):

This acclaimed festival attracts cinephiles from around the world, screening a diverse lineup of acclaimed international and Greek films against the backdrop of the island's stunning scenery.

- Amaltheia Gastronomy Festival (October):

Celebrating the culinary heritage of Rhodes, this festival features cooking demonstrations, tastings, and workshops that showcase the island's renowned local produce, olive oils, and wines.

- Traditional Village Festivals:

Throughout the autumn months, many of Rhodes' charming villages host their own local festivals, offering visitors the chance to immerse themselves in traditional music, dance, and cuisine.

These are just a few examples of the rich cultural tapestry that unfolds across Rhodes during the spring and autumn seasons. By attending these festivals and events, travelers can gain a deeper appreciation for the island's history, customs, and vibrant communities, creating lasting memories of their time in this enchanting Mediterranean destination.

Religious Sites & Architecture

From the towering Byzantine churches to the elegant Ottoman mosques, the island of Rhodes boasts a rich tapestry of religious architecture that reflects the diverse cultural influences that have shaped its history.

One of the island's most iconic religious landmarks is the magnificent **Knights of St. John Grand Master's Palace** in the medieval Old Town of Rhodes. This magnificent structure, which once served as the seat of the **Knights Hospitaller**, is a stunning example of Gothic and Byzantine architectural styles, with its ornate facades, grand halls, and impressive fortifications.

Venture beyond the Old Town and explore the island's Byzantine heritage at the Kamiros Basilica, a well-preserved early Christian church that dates back to the 5th century AD. Marvel at the intricate mosaics that adorn the floors and walls, and imagine the generations of worshippers who have walked these sacred halls.

For a glimpse into Rhodes' Ottoman legacy, visit the **Süleymaniye Mosque**, a striking example of Islamic architecture that stands as a testament to the island's multicultural history. Admire the elegant domes, the ornate mihrab (prayer niche), and the tranquil courtyard, all of which reflect the architectural traditions of the Ottoman Empire.

But the island's religious sites are not just architectural wonders; they are also hubs of spiritual and cultural significance. Engage with the local communities, attend religious services, and immerse yourself in the rituals and traditions that have been practiced here for centuries, deepening your understanding and appreciation of the island's rich and diverse religious heritage.

Whether you're a history buff, an architecture enthusiast, or simply someone in search of a deeper cultural experience, the religious sites and architecture of Rhodes offer a captivating window into the island's past and present.

Chapter 8: TRADITIONAL ARTS AND CRAFTS OF RHODES FOR TOURISTS

Visitors to Rhodes have a wonderful opportunity to immerse themselves in the island's rich tradition of arts and crafts during their stay. Here are some of the best ways to engage with this cultural heritage:

✓ **Visit the Old Town Artisan Workshops**

- The medieval Old Town of Rhodes is home to a variety of traditional workshops, where visitors can observe local artisans at work and even participate in hands-on demonstrations.

- Highlights include ceramic studios, where master potters create the iconic Rhodes pottery, as well as workshops specializing in embroidery, metalsmithing, and other time-honored crafts.

- Many of these workshops offer the chance to try your hand at creating your own piece, providing an authentic, memorable experience.

✓ **Attend Artisan Festivals and Demonstrations**

- Throughout the spring and autumn seasons, Rhodes hosts a number of festivals and events that celebrate the island's rich artisanal traditions.

- The Rhodes Medieval Festival, for example, features demonstrations of medieval crafts like blacksmithing, glassblowing, and weaving, allowing visitors to learn about the techniques that have been passed down for generations.

- Other events, such as the Amaltheia Gastronomy Festival, may include workshops on traditional food preservation methods, olive oil production, and more.

✓ Explore Local Art Galleries and Shops

- Rhodes is home to a vibrant community of contemporary artists and artisans who draw inspiration from the island's heritage.

- Visitors can browse galleries and shops throughout the island, discovering unique handmade ceramics, textiles, woodcarvings, and other works that reflect the Rhodian aesthetic.

- Many of these establishments also offer the opportunity to meet the artists and learn about their creative processes.

✓ Take a Hands-On Workshop or Class

- For a more immersive experience, visitors can enroll in specialized workshops or classes to learn traditional Rhodian crafts firsthand.

- Options may include pottery throwing, weaving, embroidery, or even traditional Greek cooking, led by experienced local instructors.

- These interactive sessions provide an opportunity to create your own meaningful souvenir while gaining a deeper appreciation for the island's artistic legacy.

By engaging with Rhodes' vibrant arts and crafts scene, visitors can forge a personal connection to the island's cultural heritage and take home a piece of its timeless artistry.

Chapter 9: MUST-VISIT ARTISAN GALLERIES IN THE OLD TOWN OF RHODES

The Old Town of Rhodes is home to a wealth of exceptional artisan shops and galleries that showcase the island's rich cultural heritage. Here are some must-visit destinations for travelers looking to immerse themselves in Rhodian arts and crafts:

Ceramics Studios

- **Coralli Ceramics:** This family-run studio has been creating the iconic Rhodes pottery for over a century, using traditional techniques and hand-painted designs.

- **Apolonia Ceramics:** Specializing in intricate, hand-painted ceramic plates, vases, and decorative pieces, this workshop offers visitors the chance to watch the artists at work.

Textile Workshops

- **Rhodian Embroidery:** Dedicated to preserving the centuries-old tradition of Rhodian embroidery, this shop features exquisitely crafted textiles, from table linens to traditional costumes.

- **Katarina's Weaving Studio:** Visitors can observe the master weavers of this studio as they create vibrant, handwoven rugs, pillows, and other textiles.

Metal and Woodworking Shops

- **Porfyris Metalwork:** This family-owned workshop has been creating intricate, handcrafted metalwork, including religious icons, jewelry, and household items, for generations.

- **Christos Woodcarving:** Specializing in traditional Rhodian woodcarvings, this shop offers an array of beautifully detailed sculptures, furniture, and decorative pieces.

Fine Art Galleries

- **Gallery Lithos:** Showcasing the work of contemporary Rhodian artists, this gallery features paintings, sculptures, and photography that capture the island's natural beauty and cultural essence.

- **Rodos Art Gallery:** Representing a diverse range of local and regional artists, this gallery offers a curated selection of paintings, ceramics, and other artworks inspired by the Aegean region.

Heritage Shops

- **The Old Town Shop:** This charming store features a wide selection of locally produced crafts, including handmade soaps, olive oil products, and traditional Rhodian sweets and preserves.

- **Erofili Herbal:** Dedicated to the island's rich botanical heritage, this shop offers an array of natural, artisanal products, from essential oils to herbal teas.

By visiting these exceptional artisan shops and galleries in the Old Town of Rhodes, travelers can discover the island's vibrant artistic traditions, engage with local creators, and bring home unique, handcrafted souvenirs that capture the essence of this enchanting Mediterranean destination.

Chapter 10: CONCLUSION - RHODES, AN ENDURING ISLAND TREASURE

Reflections on the Island's Captivating Essence

As the final pages of your Rhodes adventure draw to a close, a profound sense of wonder and appreciation fills your heart. This enchanting island has left an indelible mark, captivating your senses and etching itself into the very fabric of your memories.

From the moment you first set foot in the UNESCO-protected Medieval Old Town, you were transported back through the centuries, bearing witness to the living tapestry of history that unfolds around every cobblestone street and towering fortification. The grand palaces, ornate churches, and bustling market squares have sparked your imagination, allowing you to glimpse the resilience and ingenuity of those who have called Rhodes home for millennia.

Yet, Rhodes is not merely a relic of the past; it is an island that celebrates the vibrant present and embraces the promise of the future. In the workshops and studios of local artisans, you have encountered a profound reverence for tradition, as skilled hands craft pottery, weave textiles, and sculpt metal and wood with unparalleled mastery. These encounters have provided a profound connection to the island's cultural heritage, and have inspired a newfound appreciation for the enduring creativity of the Rhodian people.

Beyond the historical tapestry, Rhodes has captivated you with its stunning natural beauty. From the serene beaches that kiss the crystalline waters of the Aegean to the lush, butterfly-filled valleys and the dramatic, rugged coastlines, this island's landscapes have left an indelible impression. Whether you've explored these natural wonders through invigorating hikes, exhilarating water sports, or leisurely cycling tours, you have discovered a deep appreciation for the island's diverse ecosystems and the importance of preserving its fragile environments.

Inspiration to Return and Explore Further

The captivating essence of Rhodes has left an indelible mark on your heart and mind, and you find yourself longing to return to this enchanting island, to delve deeper into its cultural riches and uncover the countless hidden gems that still await your discovery.

The memories you've made and the connections you've forged with the Rhodian people have inspired a profound sense of curiosity and a desire to continue exploring the island's multifaceted cultural heritage. You yearn to revisit the workshops and studios of the island's talented artisans, to learn more about the techniques and traditions that have been passed down through generations. You're eager to venture beyond the well-trodden paths and discover the lesser-known religious sites and architectural marvels that have yet to reveal their secrets.

Your culinary journey through Rhodes has been equally revelatory, as you've indulged in the fresh seafood, the tantalizing local dishes, and the simple yet flavorful staples of the Mediterranean diet. Each bite has transported you to a world of vibrant flavors, seamlessly blending the island's agricultural heritage with the bounty of the surrounding seas.

All these must have ignited a burning desire to return, to savor the subtleties and nuances that you may have missed during your previous visits.

Preserving the Legacy of Rhodes

As you prepare to depart this enchanting island, you do so with a renewed sense of wonder and appreciation. The memories you have forged, the connections you have made, and the experiences you have savored will continue to resonate long after your return home. Rhodes has emerged not merely as a destination, but as a living, breathing testament to the enduring power of human creativity, resilience, and the timeless allure of the Mediterranean spirit.

In the years to come, you may see yourself as an ambassador for Rhodes, sharing your experiences and insights with others and encouraging them to visit this remarkable island, to engage with its people, and to contribute to the preservation of its cultural legacy. You'll seek out opportunities to support the island's artisans and craftspeople, to amplify their voices and ensure that their timeless skills continue to be celebrated and cherished.

In the end, Rhodes stands as an enduring island treasure, inviting all who visit to immerse themselves in its captivating essence and to carry a piece of its magic within their hearts forevermore. This island's enduring legacy will undoubtedly live on, inspiring future generations to explore its wonders and to honor the enduring spirit that has defined Rhodes for millennia.

Practical Information

Dining and Nightlife

Rhodes is a culinary and nightlife paradise, offering a diverse array of dining and entertainment options to suit every taste and preference.

The island's cuisine is a delectable fusion of Mediterranean flavors, drawing inspiration from the rich cultural tapestry of the region. From traditional Greek tavernas serving up mouthwatering meze platters to upscale restaurants showcasing the finest local produce and seafood, the dining scene in Rhodes is sure to delight your palate.

Be sure to indulge in the island's renowned wines, which are produced from the unique grape varieties that thrive in the Rhodian terroir. Many wineries offer tastings and tours, providing an immersive experience into the art of winemaking.

When the sun goes down, Rhodes comes alive with a vibrant nightlife scene. The charming Old Town and the lively waterfront areas are home to an array of bars, clubs, and live music venues, offering something for every mood and taste. From laid-back cocktail lounges to energetic dance clubs, the island's nightlife caters to a diverse range of preferences.

For a more authentic cultural experience, explore the traditional Greek coffee houses and tavernas, where locals gather to socialize, share stories, and enjoy the island's rich musical heritage.

Shopping and Souvenirs

Rhodes is a shopper's paradise, offering a diverse array of local handicrafts, artisanal products, and unique souvenirs that capture the essence of the island.

The Old Town of Rhodes is a veritable treasure trove, with its narrow streets and charming alleys lined with a multitude of shops, galleries, and workshops showcasing the island's rich artisanal traditions. From intricate pottery and ceramics to delicate lace work and handwoven textiles, the Rhodian artisans take pride in their craft and are eager to share their skills with visitors.

Be sure to explore the local markets, where you can find a wide range of fresh produce, fragrant spices, and traditional delicacies. These bustling hubs are not only a great place to shop but also offer a glimpse into the daily life and culture of the Rhodian people.

For those seeking more contemporary and high-end offerings, the island's designer boutiques and galleries feature a stunning array of artwork, jewelry, and fashion items that reflect the island's rich cultural heritage and modern style.

When it comes to souvenirs, the options are endless – from handcrafted ceramics and intricate embroidered linens to locally produced olive oil, honey, and wine. These unique mementos not only make for wonderful keepsakes but also serve as a tangible reminder of the captivating essence of Rhodes.

Health and Safety

Rhodes is generally a safe and secure destination for travelers, but as with any destination, it's important to take some precautions to ensure a smooth and enjoyable trip.

When it comes to healthcare, the island has a well-developed medical infrastructure, with several hospitals and clinics offering quality care. It's recommended to research and identify the nearest medical facilities to your accommodation, just in case.

Be sure to pack any necessary medications and ensure that you have comprehensive travel insurance that covers any potential medical emergencies. It's also a good idea to familiarize yourself with the local emergency numbers and procedures.

In terms of safety, Rhodes is considered a relatively low-risk destination, but it's still important to exercise caution and common sense, especially in crowded areas or when traveling at night. Petty crime, such as pickpocketing, can occur, so it's wise to keep your valuables secure and be aware of your surroundings.

When exploring the island's natural landscapes and historic sites, be mindful of any potential hazards and follow the guidance of local authorities and signage. Some areas may have uneven terrain or require special precautions, so it's always best to research and plan accordingly.

Calendar of Events

Rhodes is alive with a vibrant calendar of events and festivals throughout the year, offering visitors a chance to immerse themselves in the island's rich cultural heritage and traditions.

One of the most prominent events is the Rhodes Medieval Festival, which takes place every September in the Old Town. This lively celebration transports visitors back in time, with reenactments, live music, and theatrical performances that showcase the island's medieval history.

The Rhodian Wine Festival, held annually in the spring, is a must-attend event for oenophiles, featuring tastings, workshops, and live entertainment that celebrate the island's thriving winemaking industry.

During the summer months, the island comes alive with a variety of music and dance festivals, showcasing the vibrant performing arts scene. From the Rhodes International Film Festival to the Aegean Jazz Festival, there's always an exciting cultural event to experience.

In the autumn, the island's agricultural heritage is celebrated through events like the Olive Oil Festival and the Honey Festival, where visitors can learn about the traditional production methods and sample the island's delectable culinary offerings.

Throughout the year, the island's religious and cultural communities also host a variety of festivals and celebrations, offering visitors a unique opportunity to engage with the local traditions and customs.

Be sure to check the island's event calendar and plan your visit accordingly to make the most of the rich cultural tapestry that Rhodes has to offer.

Chapter 11: APPENDIX

Rhodes Map

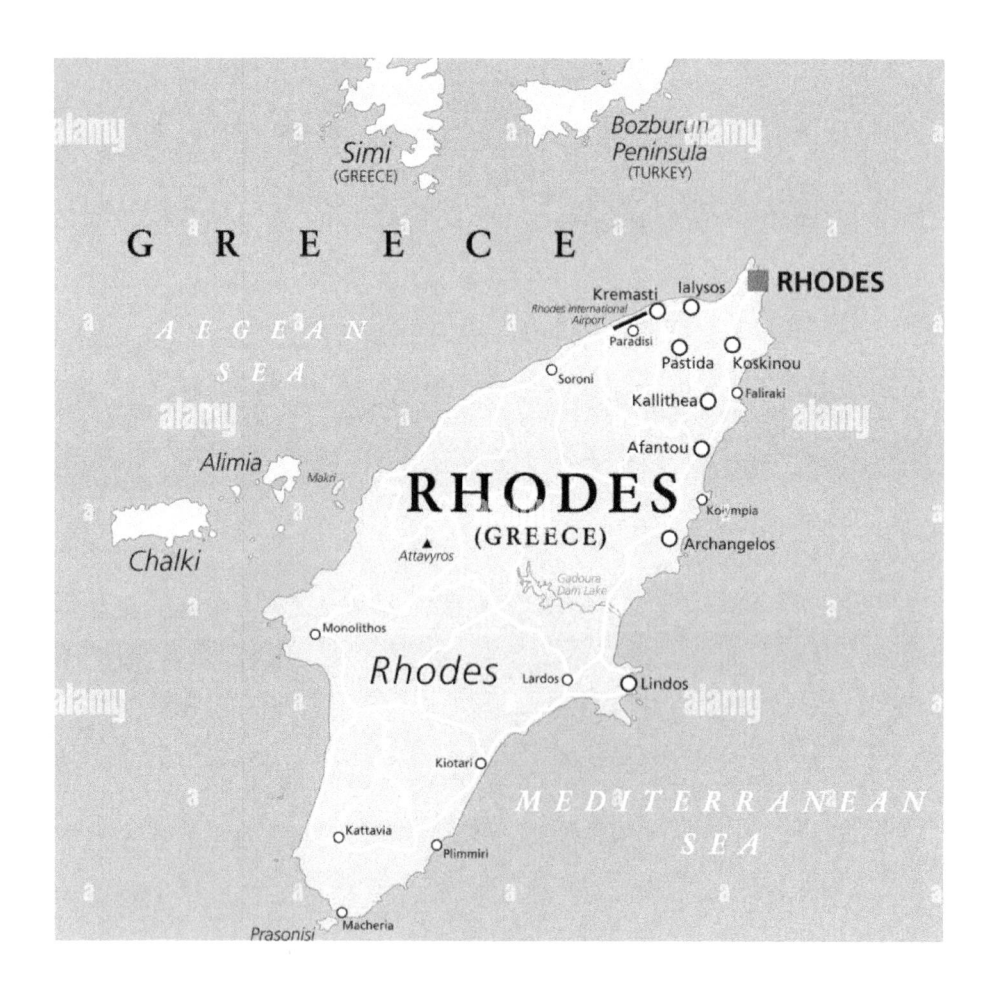

Suggested Itineraries

3-Day Itinerary

Day 1	Explore the Old Town of Rhodes, including the medieval Knights' Quarter, the Palace of the Grand Master, and the Street of the Knights. Wander through the charming alleyways, stop for a traditional Greek lunch, and visit the Archaeological Museum.
Day 2	Discover the island's natural wonders by visiting the impressive Butterfly Valley and the stunning Lindos Acropolis. In the afternoon, relax on the beaches of Lindos or Anthony Quinn Bay.
Day 3	Take a day trip to the island's lush interior, visiting the Kamiros archaeological site and the traditional village of Embonas, known for its renowned wine production. End the day with a sunset cruise along the island's picturesque coastline.

7-Day Itinerary

	Day 1-3	Explore the historic Old Town of Rhodes, the Acropolis of Lindos, and the island's beautiful beaches.
	Day 4	Venture to the northern part of the island, visiting the charming town of Kamiros Skala and the ancient ruins of Kamiros.
	Day 5	Discover the island's natural wonders, including the Butterfly Valley, the Seven Springs, and the traditional villages of Monolithos and Kritinia.
	Day 6	Spend the day in the island's interior, visiting the Epta Piges (Seven Springs) and the picturesque village of Embonas, known for its wine production.
	Day 7	Explore the eastern part of the island, visiting the town of Archangelos and the Profitis Ilias Monastery, with stunning views of the surrounding landscape.

Useful Phrases in Greek

Here are some basic Greek phrases that may be helpful during your visit to Rhodes:

GREEK PHRASES	MEANING
Γειά σου (Yiá sou)	Hello
Ευχαριστώ (Efcharistó)	Thank you
Παρακαλώ (Parakaló)	Please
Ναι (Nai)	Yes
Όχι (Óchi)	No
Πόσο κάνει; (Póso káni?)	How much?
Δεν καταλαβαίνω (Den katalaváino)	I don't understand
Μιλάτε αγγλικά; (Milate angliká?)	Do you speak English?

Additional Resources and References

Rhodes Tourism Website:

[www.rhodestourism.com] (https://www.rhodestourism.com)

Greek National Tourism Organization:

[www.visitgreece.gr] (https://www.visitgreece.gr)

Lonely Planet Guide to Rhodes:

[www.lonelyplanet.com/greece/rhodes] (https://www.lonelyplanet.com/greece/rhodes)

TripAdvisor Rhodes Forum:

[www.tripadvisor.com/Tourism-g189448-Rhodes_Dodecanese_South_Aegean-Vacations.html]

(https://www.tripadvisor.com/Tourism-g189448-Rhodes_Dodecanese_South_Aegean-Vacations.html)

Rhodes Wikipedia Page:

en.wikipedia.org/wiki/Rhodes